MR. FLEM

MUSHROOM IDENTIFICATION BOOK OF THE UK

A 4-Step Mushroom Field Guide for Identification, Harvesting, and Preparing Edible Wild Mushrooms & Wild Fungi of Britain and Europe

STEPHEN FLEMING

Disclaimer

- The objective of the book is simply to provide information; it is not intended to replace diagnosis and treatment, tasks which pertain to a doctor.

- The contents of this book are for informational purposes and are not intended to offer personal medical advice.

- You should seek the advice of your physician or another qualified health provider regarding a medical condition. Never disregard professional medical advice or delay seeking it because of something you have read in this book. The book does not recommend or endorse any products.

- Any book, video, or other means of learning can't replace learning physically from an expert. These forms of information are only additional guidance to be used along with a practical demonstration and training.

- Always check the legal status of the plant you intend to forage and use.

CHAPTERS

Introduction

What is the first thing that comes into your head when you hear the word mushrooms?

Chances are you think about chanterelle, porcini, or button mushrooms. Or maybe you start imagining little colorful images right out of a fairytale. Well, there's so much more to mushrooms than just this. Mushrooms are versatile and come in various sizes, shapes, and colors. In addition, a variety of edible mushrooms can also be found in the wild.

Have you ever noticed mushrooms cropping up on stumps and logs after a rainfall?

Have you ever wondered if all those mushrooms were edible?

If you have, then it's time to learn about foraging for mushrooms. Before you can harvest different types of edible mushrooms found in the wild, identifying them is crucial. This is needed because over a million fungi are known to us.

It is also not restricted to enhancing the nutritional profile of your meals. The role played by mushrooms in maintaining ecological balance is highly critical. They help plants obtain nutrients and moisture from the soil. As a result, all the organic matter in the soil is further broken down and turned into nutrients that plants need.

Mushrooms not only have culinary purposes but medicinal applications too. From strengthening the functioning of the immune system, fighting infections, and reducing cognitive decline to tackling inflammation, these are just some of the health benefits mushrooms offer.

United Kingdom Map

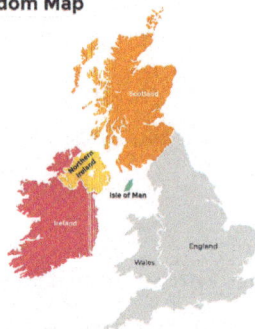

Mushroom Foraging in wild

Photo by Maria Orlova:
https://www.pexels.com/photo/crop-woman-showing-fresh-mushroom-near-river-in-forest-4906153/

If you are interested in learning to look for these ingredients in the wild, "*Mushroom Identification Book UK: A 4-Step Mushroom Field Guide for Identification, Harvesting, and Preparing Edible Wild Mushrooms in 4-Weeks in The UK*" is the perfect book for you.

Before you head outdoors to look for edible mushrooms in the wild, understand that foraging is not a new trend or fad. Instead, it is an activity that's been a part of the human lifestyle since the dawn of civilization.

Foraging and hunting were the only means through which our prehistoric ancestors obtained sustenance. Foraging collectively refers to the process of identifying, gathering, and harvesting edibles found in the wild, including plants and mushrooms.

This is not only an enjoyable physical activity but is a stressbuster, an excellent hobby, and a great way to learn about the local ecosystem too.

This is not only an enjoyable physical activity but is a stressbuster, an excellent hobby, and a great way to learn about the local ecosystem too.

The United Kingdom includes England, Wales, Scotland, and Northern Ireland. The UK, in general, has a temperate climate. Warm and wet summers coupled with cool and wet winters create the ideal environment for a variety of fungi to grow. Different types of edible mushrooms can be found in the wild in the UK. Whether they are chanterelles, morels, or boletes, there's a lot to learn and explore.

Photo by Annie Spratt on Unsplash

Foraging for mushrooms is a rewarding experience because they make a brilliant addition to any meal you want to cook. As mentioned, some mushrooms also have medicinal properties.

Before you head outdoors to look for mushrooms, it is important to understand what you are looking for, their identifying factors, and whether they are edible or not. Learning to distinguish the edible variants from their poisonous counterparts is important.

Once you know how to go about this, foraging will become exciting. The good news is you don't have to spend additional time searching for the relevant information. This book will act as your guide every step of the way. It will teach you the four simple steps you must follow to become an ethical forager.

You will also learn about identifying different edible and inedible or poisonous mushrooms commonly found in the UK. Apart from this, you will also be introduced to different recipes that can be cooked using the mushrooms you foraged.

So, are you excited to start learning more about all this? Do you want to become a mushroom forager? If yes, there is no time like the present to get started!

1. Getting Started With Mushrooms

Before you learn to become a mushroom forager, it's important to understand what mushrooms are, their general anatomy, and their various benefits. Once you are armed with this information, you will start appreciating the value of different mushrooms foraged. You think about button mushrooms, chanterelles, or morels when you hear the word mushroom.

Well, mushrooms are extremely versatile and come in a variety of shapes, sizes, and colors. As versatile as they are, their edibility and medicinal properties also vary. Some are scrumptious, while others are inedible and toxic.

MUSHROOM ANATOMY

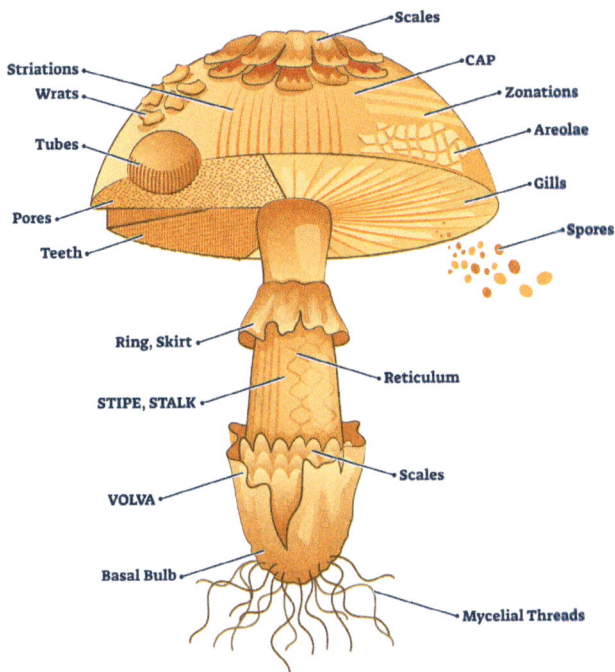

What Are Mushrooms?

The reproductive structure of certain types of fungi is known as mushrooms. Mushrooms are similar to fruits produced by plants. Plants propagate by seeds, while mushrooms have millions of microscopic pores. When the spores land on a specific substrate or food source ideal for them, they germinate and create an intricate network of interconnected rooting threads known as mycelium. After this, the fruiting body or the visible part of the mushroom pops up and is visible above ground.

Currently, tens of thousands of mushrooms are known to humanity.

However, mycologists believe this is only a fraction of all that's yet to be discovered. Mushrooms are not just a culinary delight but also an important part of the natural ecosystem.

Fungi, in general, promote the decomposition of organic matter by devouring dead and decaying matter. Certain fungi also help plants extract nutrients they require from the soil, while the mushrooms get their sustenance from the said plants. Mushrooms also have medicinal applications.

Identify The Parts Of A Mushroom

Without understanding their basic structure and life cycle, you cannot start foraging mushrooms. Learning about this gives you better insight into the types of mushrooms you are foraging and how to identify them.

The general anatomy of a mushroom includes cap, gills, spores, mycelium, stipe, ring, veil, hyphae, and volva. There is so much more to mushrooms than just the fruiting body visible above the ground. Let's learn in detail about all this.

The top part of the mushroom is known as its cap or pileus. This is the first part of the mushroom you'll notice. As the name suggests, it is an umbrella or a dome-like structure. The primary function of the cap is to protect the gills and their spores from the elements.

The area under the cap is covered with fine tooth-like structures known as gills. These are quite similar to the gills of a fish. Gills contain the pores or spores of mushrooms. Flowering and fruiting plants propagate by seeds, while mushrooms produce spores.

Mycelium refers to the root-like structure of the present mushroom underground. Mycelium not only promotes the growth of new mushrooms but ensures they obtain the desired nutrients. These are fine hair-like strands that grow underground, known as hyphae. The mushroom cap rests on a structure known as its stem or stipe. A vertical portion of the mushroom is visible above the surface.

The underside of the mushroom cap has a protective layer known as the veil. Its primary function is to keep the spores safe and secure until it matures.

Mushrooms also have a small ring-like structure known as its annulus or the ring. The annulus is the remnant of the veil present on the mushroom's stipe.

It essentially acts as an additional layer of protection that keeps the spores safe while the mushroom matures. The mushroom breaks through its veil as the cap grows.

The leftover bits of the veil form a ring around its stem. The volva is a cup-like structure close to the base of the stem, which is also a leftover bit of its veil.

All the different parts of the mushroom discussed in this section are commonly used for identifying the species. So, spend some time and acquaint yourself with the anatomy of mushrooms.

Health Benefits Of Mushrooms

Mushrooms are not only a culinary delight but also commonly used as meat substitutes. They are a powerhouse of nutrients. Apart from this, several mushrooms have medicinal properties and, therefore, are commonly used in traditional medicine by different cultures across the globe.

Foraging Mushroom with kids

Mushrooms are rich in antioxidants that reduce the risk of different types of cancer due to high levels of selenium and vitamin D. Vitamin D supplementation is known to fight certain types of cancers. Apart from this, the helpful antioxidant known as choline also does the same.

Mushrooms reduce the risk of developing type-2 diabetes and regularize blood sugar levels due to their dietary fiber. Since type-2 diabetes is a known health marker of several chronic disorders, including cardiovascular dysfunctions, adding mushrooms to your diet is a wonderful idea.

Cardiovascular health improves when your body gets its daily vitamin C, potassium, and dietary fiber. All these healthy ingredients are known to regulate blood pressure levels and reduce the risk of hypertension. Vitamin C is needed to maintain and strengthen the heart's functioning. Since all these nutrients are abundant in mushrooms, adding them to your diet can work wonders.

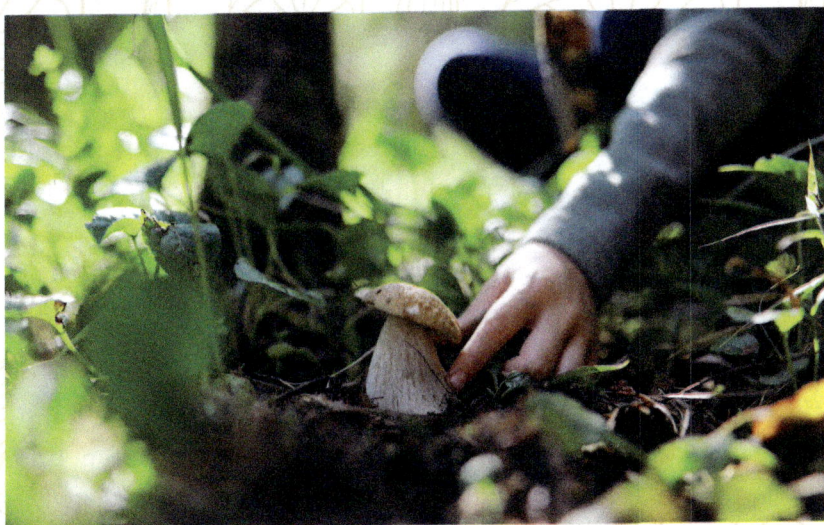

Foraging Mushroom

They are rich in antioxidants that reduce damage caused by oxidative stress. Oxidative stress is also a leading cause of aging. You can reverse all this by simply consuming more mushrooms. The antioxidants also tackle inflammation responsible for cognitive disorders. So, besides improving heart health, you can also improve cognitive functioning.

Mushrooms also have plenty of calcium and vitamin D needed to strengthen and improve your skeletal framework's function. Apart from all this, they are rich in different B-complex vitamins, minerals, and nutrients responsible for regulating your energy levels. So, adding mushrooms to your diet improves your overall health and leaves you feeling more energetic.

These health benefits offered by mushrooms are further enhanced when you start foraging for them in the wild. Foraging is a great way to start spending more time outdoors and connecting with nature. An important aspect of foraging is understanding the local ecosystem.

These insights will automatically make you more aware of the problems the environment is facing. A combination of these factors increases the inclination to make environmentally friendly choices. Foraging is also a great hobby. If you've been looking for a new hobby, start foraging today.

To become a forager, you need an open mindset, a curious mind, and a willingness to learn. All the information you gather can also be shared with others. Foraging can become an engaging family activity. This can also be your reason for disconnecting from regular life and reducing your stress levels.

2. Four Steps to Forage Mushrooms

Learning to forage mushrooms is an enriching activity. It is also an excellent opportunity to learn and become a lifelong learner. There are only four simple steps you should follow to start foraging mushrooms. With dedication, commitment, and consistency, you can start foraging mushrooms within 4-weeks.

Step 1: Learn

The first step of becoming a mushroom forager is to keep an open mind to learning. There is a lot to learn, and never make the mistake of believing that you know everything. Foraging is not restricted to just picking mushrooms in the wild. It's also about understanding how they grow, their properties, and what can be done with them. Foraging by itself is an engaging and exciting activity that gives you a chance to get away from the urban jungle and spend some time reconnecting with nature. Please don't go with the sole goal of picking mushrooms when it comes to foraging. Instead, think of every experience as a learning opportunity.

Foraging

When learning about mushrooms, you should familiarize yourself with their basic anatomy. It would help if you also learned about the common seasons or months during which certain mushrooms are found. Mushrooms are not like Evergreen shrubs. Instead, some sprout only in certain conditions. You will find a detailed calendar for different mushrooms commonly found in the UK.

While learning about mushrooms, remember that some are gourmet delicacies while others are inedible and downright poisonous. If you are residing in the UK — the regions of England, Northern Ireland, Scotland, and Wales be prepared to come across different species of mushrooms.

This book introduces you to the basic information required to identify common mushroom species in the UK. There's a lot included, from learning about their cap size and color to the general appearance and other identifying factors.

Step 2: Identify

Learning to identify mushrooms is an art in itself. When it comes to foraging, you must be 100% certain of the mushroom you want to harvest. As a rule of thumb, avoiding a species you're unsure of is always better. There will be a variety of edible mushrooms you come across, and at the same time, there will be some poisonous varieties too.

To identify a mushroom, you must consider its cap shape and size, spores, and stem. These three characteristics help ascertain whether a specific mushroom is what you think it is or not.

Mushrooms come in a variety of shapes and sizes. This means the shape and size, and caps also vary. Apart from this, you should also pay attention to its color and texture. Whenever you come across a mushroom, could you take note of its color or colors?

After this, make a note of the original color too. The color usually changes as the mushroom matures. When cut or bruised, the cap color changes upon exposure to air. This applies to the flesh of mushrooms too. It would help if you also looked for any general markings that are unusual or specific to a mushroom family. In some cases, looking at the cap's edge is another indicator.

Spores

Magnifying Glass

After the cap, move on to identifying the spores of the mushroom. You'll find the spores on the underside of the cap.

The gills are, at times, attached to the stem. In other cases, they are not. Pay attention to the consistency, color, and thickness of the gills. Apart from it, look at the shape and color of the spores. To do this, you should always carry a magnifying glass.

After this, the next step is to examine its stem. Pay extra attention to the stem's shape, color, and size. Is the stem thick, short, or thin?

Is its color consistent with the color of the cap you noticed? See whether there is a ring or an annulus on the stem. Look for any other external markings, such as freckles. Also, examine how the stem is connected to the soil.

Once you have noted all the points mentioned until now, crosscheck whether the mushroom at hand matches the description of what it is supposed to be or not. Even if you have a little doubt, stay away from the species. It's always better to be extra cautious when it comes to mushrooms. Some might look harmless, but they can be poisonous. In the subsequent chapters, you will learn about the different features that can be used for identifying edible and poisonous mushrooms in the UK.

Step 3: Harvest

Once you have identified a mushroom, it's vital to ensure that you have eliminated all traces of doubt. A famous saying among mushroom foragers goes like this, "there are either old mushroom hunters or bold mushroom hunters."

This is because incorrectly or wrongly identifying a mushroom can prove to be a fatal mistake. Ensure that you are not one of the fatalities. The symptoms of mushroom poisoning can vary from physical discomfort to death because of no known antidotes.

Once you have checked and rechecked the mushroom you wish to forage; the next stage is harvesting it. Harvesting a mushroom is not just about plucking it off the forest floor. It would help if you didn't gather mushrooms haphazardly.

Basket & Knife
Basket & Knife

Much care is needed because mushrooms are pretty delicate and get bruised easily. This can alter their flavor profile. Also, you should not disturb the entire natural setting just to college a few mushrooms.

As a rule of thumb, ensure you never disturb the smallest 50% of the mushrooms you find in a patch. If there are only one or two patches of a specific species, avoid foraging them.

Also, ensure that the species you are foraging are neither endangered nor at risk. It would help if you always left a few mushrooms behind for a specific species so they can grow, ripen, and propagate.

This is one rule all ethical foragers must follow. Along the same lines, never harvest more than what you need. After all, you are not the only forager. Also, humans are not the only ones fond of mushrooms, so consider the local fauna.

The two standard methods used for foraging mushrooms are cutting and picking. Picking is a simple method to pluck the mushroom off the ground carefully.

Depending on the species of mushroom, the method will differ. For instance, the ideal technique for foraging morels is cutting while plucking works for boletes. Any species of mushroom that you can identify quickly can be cut. This ensures the mycelium is not disturbed and that future growth is not hindered. On the other hand, certain mushrooms have to be identified rather carefully, including identifying their mycelium. In such instances, uproot the entire mushroom carefully.

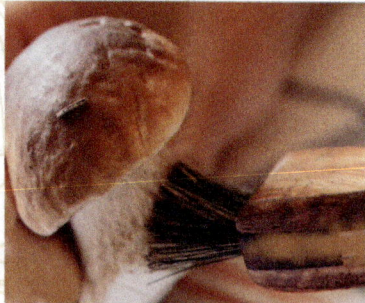

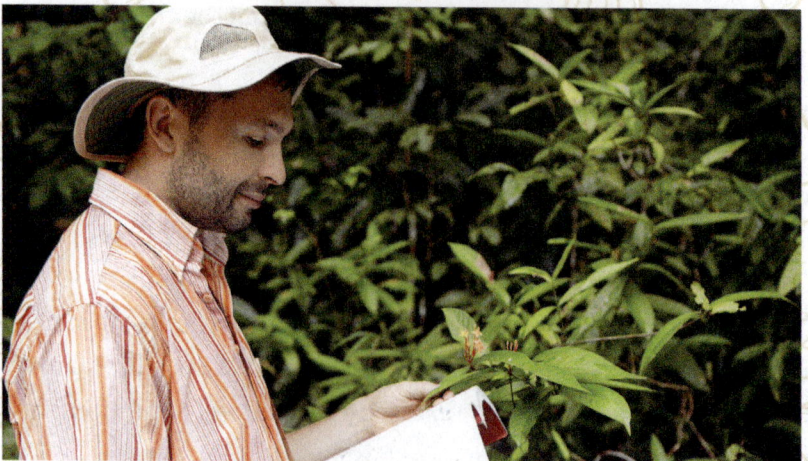

Brush, Magnifying Glass & Field Guide

Step 4: Preserve & Prepare

As an ethical forager, your job doesn't end with foraging the mushrooms you need. Instead, it includes the additional step of enjoying the mushrooms you foraged. After all, foraging is not a simple task and takes time and effort. Mushrooms are delicious and nutritious.

Their texture, taste, and flavor can quickly elevate the flavor profile of any dish you cook. Whether it is pasta, soup, stew, or a salad, mushrooms can be incorporated into any dish. Some taste wonderful when simply sautéed or grilled with butter and seasonings. Learning to prepare mushrooms is important to ensure that their minerals and helpful nutrients are not lost.

The good news is that you don't have to spend additional time searching for recipes that use wild edible mushrooms. This book includes a variety of simple and delicious recipes you can cook using foraged mushrooms. All these recipes are not only easy but simple to cook as well. Apart from preparing the mushrooms for immediate consumption, some can be preserved too.

The most common techniques for preserving mushrooms include drying and freezing. Clean the foraged mushrooms thoroughly and recheck to ensure you have not accidentally picked inedible or poisonous varieties.

Once the mushrooms are thoroughly cleaned with water, gently pat them dry. After this, leave them out to dry under the sun.

Alternatively, you can also use a dehydrator for this. The dehydrated mushrooms must be stored in an airtight container and kept away from direct sunlight. Simply add the dehydrated mushrooms to any soup or stew of your choice.

Another method for preserving mushrooms is freezing. The cleaned mushrooms, place them in freezer-friendly airtight containers or bags such as ziplock bags. After this, place them in the freezer! When stored properly, they can last for over six months. Mushrooms have high water content. This means that when frozen, their texture is slightly altered.

Preserving Mushroom

3. Let's Meet Common Wild Mushrooms

Common Edible Mushrooms Identification

(1) Horse Mushroom

Horse mushroom or Agaricus Arvensis is a delicious mushroom with a rich and strong taste. These mushrooms can be found in meadows, pastures, road verges, lawns, and parks. They usually grow in rings. The average width of the cap and height of the stem is 25 and 10 centimeters, respectively. They usually have smooth or, at times, scaly white caps. Young mushrooms have a spherical cap that opens up as they mature. The gills in the young ones are white, which turns pinkish-grey or brown when they mature. Their stout stem has a double ring with a fairly large skirt that shrinks away. They have ellipsoidal spores, which are dark brown or purple. Their aroma is reminiscent of aniseed and makes a wonderful addition to savory dishes

Horse Mushrooms

Image by Janet Herman from Pixabay

(2) Prince Mushroom

The prince or Agaricus Augustus is an excellent fleshy mushroom that smells of bitter almonds. They are commonly found in mixed forests, especially under conifers. You will also find them along roadsides.

While picking them, ensure you forage from areas away from urban spaces. The spherical cap of young mushrooms turns convex as they mature.

The average width of the cap and height of the stem is 20 and 20 centimeters, respectively. The cap by itself is pale yellow or white, covered with concentric scales that are chestnut brown colored.

As they mature, the off-white gills turn pink and dark brown. The gills are crowded and not attached to the stem. The stem is pale, cream-colored, and smooth. It is also covered with small brown scales below its large pendulous skirt. Their ellipsoidal spores are purple or chocolate brown colored.

Prince Mushroom or Agaricus Augustus

(3) Pavement Mushrooms

As the name suggests, pavement mushrooms or Agaricus Bitorquis can grow through asphalt and dry compact soil. This means you'll find them growing beside roads and paths.

The mushroom's average height and cap width are 7 and 15 centimeters, respectively. When young, they start with a white and convex cap that flattens out in mature species. The cap is usually covered in mud and dust, so you must thoroughly clean it.

The white or grey gills turn pink or dark brown when fully mature. The gills are not joined to the stem and are crowded. Its white stem is stout and tapers at the base. The double edge skirt of this mushroom is another identifying feature.

The sub-globose spores are brown in color. These mushrooms have a strong heady aroma and should be fully cooked before consumption.

Agaricus Bitorquis

(4) Medusa Mushroom

Medusa mushroom or Agaricus bohusii was initially considered rare but has become quite common in the UK over the last decade. They usually grow in dense clusters.

These mushrooms can be commonly found under trees in mixed-wood forests and parks. The mushroom's average height and its cap's widths are 15 and 20 centimeters, respectively. These mushrooms have a firm cap with triangular scales. These scales are distinctly pointed and raised above the surface.

As the mushrooms pass through the ground, their surface is often covered in soil, and you will need to pay extra attention to identify them. The gills on these mushrooms are pale pink or white, to begin with, and slowly turn dark brown. The crowded gills are free from its stem. The long stems of these mushrooms have a pointy base, and the mushrooms grow in joined clusters at the base. The stem is white, to begin with, and slowly turns brown. You might also notice scales below the ring. The flesh of these mushrooms is pristine white but quickly turns reddish-brown when exposed to air. The ellipsoidal spores are black or dark brown colored.

Medusa mushroom or Agaricus bohusii

(5) Field Mushroom

Field mushrooms or Agaricus Campestris can be commonly found in parks, pastures, lawns, and meadows across the United Kingdom. The mushroom's average height and its cap's widths are 8 and 10 centimeters, respectively.

When young, the cap of this mushroom is spherical. It's usually white but is, at times, discolored and takes on a grey-brown hue. The cap can be either smooth or scaly. When bruised, it takes on a pinkish hue.

A good indicator of a field mushroom is its cuticle hanging down over the cap's rim. The deep pink gills turn dark brown when they mature. The gills are attached to the stem and are crowded. The stem is white and smooth above the ring and slightly scaly below it. Usually, you might not even find traces of this ring because it's delicate. The ovoid spores are chocolate brown colored.

Field mushrooms or Agaricus Campestris

(6) Scaly Wood Mushroom

The Scaly Wood Mushroom, or Agaricus Langei, is also known as the great wood mushroom. These mushrooms are commonly found in open mixed woodlands or forests. The mushroom's average height and cap width are 10 centimeters each.

When young, the cap is vertical and becomes convex as the mushroom matures. You will notice slightly reddish-brown scales that appear concentrically. The cap itself is white or pale yellow colored. The gills are crowded but not attached to the stem.

They start pink and turn dark brown as the mushroom matures. The stem is white or pale cream-colored with red tints and brown skills. The ellipsoidal spores are purple and brown. Also, this mushroom smells like almonds.

Scaly Wood Mushroom, or Agaricus Langei

(7) The Blushing Wood Mushroom

The blushing wood mushroom, or Agaricus Silvaticus, is also known as the scaly wood mushroom and Pinewood Mushroom. These mushrooms can be commonly found in coniferous forests but sometimes grow under deciduous trees. The mushroom's average height and its cap's widths are 8 and 10 centimeters, respectively.

The spherical cap of young mushrooms becomes convex when fully mature. It starts with brown fiber-like lines that turn into small scales. If the cap is damaged or bruised, it quickly turns a bright red shade.

The crowded off-white gills become grey or a reddish-dark brown as the mushroom grows. The grey stipe of the mature mushrooms is usually white when young. The stem also has a bulbous base. It has brown-colored ovoid spores.

Agaricus Silvaticus

(8) Wood Mushroom

Wood mushrooms or Agaricus Silvicola are commonly found in mixed woodlands across the United Kingdom. These mushrooms are fairly common and have a strong aniseed smell. Ensure you consume these mushrooms on the same day because they go bad quickly. The mushroom's average height and its cap's widths are 8 and 10 centimeters, respectively.

They have flat caps that are spherical, to begin with. The off-white or cream caps become yellowish with age. The pale grey or pink gills turn dark chocolate brown as a mushroom matures.

The stem has a bulbous base and is white or off-white. It also has a pendulous ring, and its surface is usually stained with spores. The ellipsoidal spores of this mushroom are purple or brown colored.

Wood mushrooms or Agaricus Silvicola

(9) Orange Peel Fungus

Orange peel fungus or aleuria aurantia doesn't have a distinct cap. And instead, it has tiers of corrugated flesh that come together to form a rosette.

It almost looks like a pretty flower with multiple petals. They usually grow flat on the ground or might be a few centimeters off the ground if a stem is present. The average height and width of the cap are 5 and 10 centimeters, respectively. The sports of this mushroom are not visible to the naked eye but are present on the upper surface of the capital cell.

They don't have a stem per se and, instead, have a short thickening around the middle of the cap. The flesh of this mushroom is the same color as the underside of its cap.

They are commonly found on gravel soil or grass near roads. These mushrooms have ellipsoidal white-colored spores. These mushrooms are extremely common in the UK.

Orange peel fungus or aleuria aurantia
Image by PublicDomainPictures from Pixabay

(10) Orange Grisette

Orange grisette or amanita crocea is also known as saffron ringless amanita. They are commonly found in coniferous forests, especially birch or beech trees. These mushrooms are quite pretty.

The average height and width of the cap are 14 and 10 centimeters, respectively. Initially, these mushrooms have an egg-shaped cap that slowly opens out and becomes almost flat.

As the mushroom matures, it takes on a bright orange color. You will notice radial striations toward the edge of the cap. It has crowded off-white gills.

The pale orange stem has a snakeskin pattern on it. It has an extremely thick, white, and long volval sac close to its base. The subglobose spores of this mushroom a white-colored.

Orange grisette or amanita crocea

(11) The Blusher

The blusher or amanita rubescens is a common mushroom found in mixed woodlands across the United Kingdom. The average height and width of the cap are 15 centimeters each, respectively.

This mushroom initially has a spherical cap that slowly turns convex and becomes flat as it matures. Its flesh-colored cap can take on a dark brown or red hue with yellow tints as it matures. Its white gills are quite crowded and free of the stem. If damaged, these gills develop red spots. It has off-white-grey scales on the stem. The skirt is an important feature for identifying this mushroom.

Look for fine grooves or striations that run along the length of the skirt. This mushroom has pristine white flesh that quickly turns red when exposed to air or bruised. It has ovoid white-colored spores.

Blusher or Amanita Rubescensol
Image by Andreas from Pixabay

(12) Grisettes

Grisette or Amanita vaginata is essentially a ringless amanita mushroom. These mushrooms are commonly found in woodlands with broad-leaved or coniferous trees and next to herbaceous plants as well.

The average height and width of the cap are 8-15 and 4-12 centimeters, respectively. Most grisettes have a white cap that slowly flattens out but retains an umbo even when fully mature.

The color of the cap can be pure white, beige, or even brown-grey. Regardless of the color, they have a darker center and striations along the edge of the cap.

The usually white- or cream-colored gills are crowded and free from the stem. The stem is also the same color as the cap. At times, you might notice a snakeskin pattern on it. It has spherical white spores.

Grisette or Amanita vaginata

30

(13) Honey Fungus

Honey fungus, or armillaria mellea, is a delicious mushroom. It should always be tried in small amounts because it can upset the stomach, especially for those with digestive disorders.

The average height and width of the cap are 14 and 15 centimeters, respectively. These mushrooms usually grow in large clusters on stumps or trunks of deadwood.

The conical cap of young mushrooms turns convex as they mature and has upturned edges. As the name suggests, it is the color of honey or a pleasant shade of ochre. The center of the mushroom is slightly elevated and is of a darker color than the rest of the cap.

You might also notice concentric circles made of dark scales on the cap. As the mushroom matures, the white cap slowly takes on a yellow or brown hue. These crowded gills are also joined to the stem. These mushrooms have a fairly thick and scaly white-yellow brown stem. The stem is thin, close to the top, and bulbous at the base. These mushrooms have a skirt placed relatively high on the stem, which might seem like a double ring. They have ellipsoidal white or pale-cream-colored spores.

Honey Fungus
Image by Else Siegel from Pixabay

(14) Wood/Jelly ear,

Wood ears or auricularia auricula-judae are prevalent species of mushrooms found throughout the year across the United Kingdom. They prefer dead or living elder trees and grow in clusters. They are also known as Jelly ears or tree ear mushrooms.

They do not have a stem per see, and the average width of the cap is around 5 centimeters.

Instead, the mushroom has a fruiting body shaped like an ear, hence the name. The fruiting body is covered with extremely fine hair-like structures and can be brown-red or tan-colored.

The pores are present on the underside of the fruiting body. It has jelly-like translucent flesh. These interesting mushrooms have sausage-shaped white-colored spores.

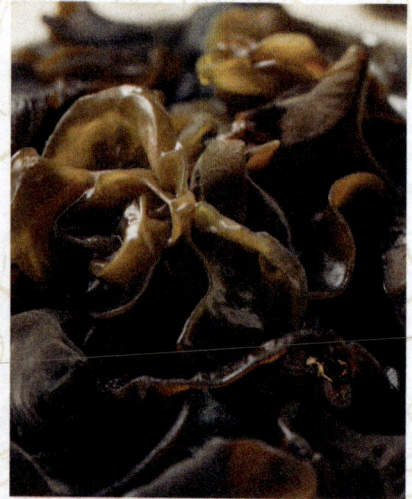

Image by Gemshots from Pixabay

Wood/Jelly Ear

(15) Butter Bolete

Butter bolete or butyriboletus appendiculatus is a large mushroom with a firm texture.

These mushrooms are commonly found near deciduous trees but usually prefer oak. The average height and width of the cap are 12 and 20 centimeters, respectively.

These mushrooms have an almost flat rusty or reddish-brown cap. The coloring on the cap is usually irregular, and it might have a cracked appearance, especially near the center.

They have tight sponge-like pores, a bright lemon yellow that darkens as the mushroom matures. It has a club-shaped or a straight stem lemon yellow colored stamp.

Sometimes, you might notice a net-like or mesh covering on the stem. The stammers read towards the base and yellow toward the top. The sub-fusiform spores are brown colored.

Butter bolete or butyriboletus appendiculatus

(16) Peppery Bolete

As the name suggests, peppery boletes or chalciporus piperatus taste pepper-like. When dried, they can be turned into a powder and used just like pepper for seasoning. These mushrooms are commonly found close to pine or birch trees.

The average height and width of the cap are 7 and 8 centimeters, respectively. This mushroom has convex caps that flatten and cracks with age. It looks shiny but is dry to the touch. The color of the cap can be cinnamon or brown.

It has a fairly thin stem, given that it belongs to the bolete family. The stem itself is yellow or cinnamon-colored with vertical striations. It has yellow flesh too. Their ellipsoidal spores are cinnamon-colored.

Peppery Boletes

(17) Summer Bolete

Summer bolete or boletus reticulatus is also known as the summer cep. These mushrooms are incredibly delicious and easy to find during summer in the UK.

These mushrooms are commonly found in broadleaved forests, close to oak and beech trees. The cap is flat, starts with a velvety texture, and becomes finely cracked when mature. It also goes from a pale brown to a brownish-yellow.

The average height and width of the cap are 15 and 15 centimeters, respectively. It has a barrel-like off-white-colored stem that is slightly lighter closer to the cap.

The flesh is white, to begin with, and takes on a yellow tinge as the mushroom matures. The sub-fusiform spores are brown colored.

Summer bolete or boletus reticulatus

(18) Giant Puffball

Giant puffball or Calvatia Gigantea is one of the safest mushrooms any forager can begin with. They are also quite easy to spot. These mushrooms essentially look like golf balls and grow in rings.

At times, they also bloom solitarily. You'll commonly find them in pastures, lawns, grasslands, and even roadsides. The mushroom barley has a stem, usually connected to the ground with its mycelium.

The fruiting body is large and can be up to 80 centimeters wide. Initially, the white or off-white colored cap has a dome-like surface that becomes smooth like paper as the mushroom matures.

As the mushroom matures, the white flash also takes on a yellowish-brown tinge. These common mushrooms have spherical yellow-brown colored spores.

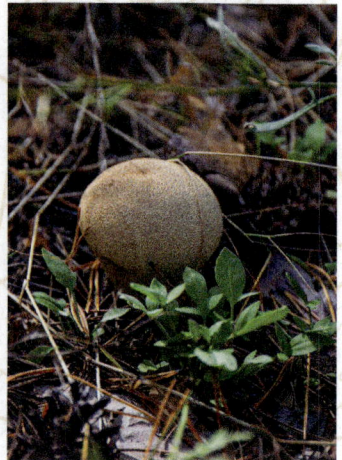

Image by DomenicBlair from Pixabay

Giant Puffball

(19) Chanterelle

Chanterelle or Cantharellus cibarius is a delicious mushroom commonly found in open woodlands and near beech or birch trees. These mushrooms grow in patches and have an average height and cap width of 10 centimeters each.

The young mushrooms have a flat cap with irregular margins. As the mushroom matures, it takes a trumpet-like shape with depression and its center. They do not have bladed gills but rounded folds that look like gills. The stem is quite solid and tapers close to the base. It has a white flash with yellow tints. These mushrooms have a fruity smell similar to apricots and are a gastronomic delight. Its ellipsoidal spores are ochre-colored.

Chanterelle

Image by Barbroforsberg from Pixabay

(20) Horn Of Plenty

Horn of plenty or craterellus cornucopioides is also known as the black trumpet mushrooms. These delicious mushrooms usually grow in clusters.

These mushrooms prefer woodland forests and grow under leaf litter. So, carefully check the forest floor if you are looking for this species. They usually grow in clusters under beech trees. The average height and width of the cap are 7 and 5 centimeters, respectively.

These mushrooms do not have a demarcated cap or stem. Instead, they have a funnel or a trumpet-shaped fruiting body with uneven edges. These mushrooms can be brown, grey, or black colored. They don't have true gills but slight ridges that run from the edge of the cap and down the stem.

These ridges are also grey-brown colored. The stem is brown-colored and hollow. The ellipsoidal spores are cream, salmon, or yellow-colored.

Horn of Plenty or Craterellus Cornucopioides

(21) Winter Chanterelle

Winter Chanterelles or Craterellus Tubaeformis are tasty mushrooms that grow solitarily or in groups with conifers. They usually grow during the winter months. The fruiting body of these chanterelles is 2-7 centimeters wide with a brownish-yellow cap.

The cap has a depressed center giving them a funnel-like appearance. The cap's margins are wavy and irregular. When fresh, these mushrooms are sticky to touch. As with other chanterelles, even they have cross-veined and forked gills extending downward from the top of the stem.

When young, the stem has a yellowish-orange hue and takes on a brownish tinge as it matures. The stem is hollow and can be 3-9 centimeters long. The elliptical spores are white or pale yellow colored. The deep depression in the mushroom cap makes them look like exotic tropical flowers.

They are rich in a variety of B-complex vitamins known for reducing inflammation, promoting bone health, and reducing the risk of diabetes. They are also rich in potassium, phosphorus, iron, and healthy dietary fiber.

Winter Chanterelles or Craterellus Tubaeformis

(22) Shaggy Ink Cap

Shaggy inky cap or Coprinus comatus are also known as judge wig and lawyer wig. These are extremely delicious mushrooms but have an incredibly short shelf life. So, ensure that they are consumed on the same day as foraged.

You can commonly find these mushrooms by the side of roads and areas where the soil is disturbed, such as grasslands and lawns. The average height and width of the cap are 40 and 15 centimeters, respectively. They have long cylindrical finger-shaped caps that take on a conical shape as the mushroom matures. The cap's color is white or off-white, to begin with, and slowly turns greyish black. You might also notice a pink tinge on it. It has tan scales too. The gills go from white to pink and ultimately black as they start melting from the edges and fuse themselves with the stem.

The long, narrow, hollow stem has a slightly swollen base and is white-colored. It has white flesh. Its ellipsoidal spores are blackish-brown colored.

Shaggy inky cap/lawyer wig

(23) Beefsteak Fungus

Beefsteak fungus or Fistulina hepatica is also known as ox tongue fungus due to its appearance. These mushrooms are incredibly delicious and meaty. They can also be used as a meat substitute. These mushrooms usually grow on living or dead oak and chestnut trees.

They do not have a discernible stem per se, and the cap can be up to 20 centimeters wide. The tongue or liver-shaped cap has an inflated edge that flattens out as the mushroom grows. Its cap can be red, reddish-pink, or reddish-brown colored. It is moist or sticky to the touch. It has tiny round tubules or pores that are off-white or cream-colored.

It has an extremely short and thick lateral stem if a stem is present. The flesh of these mushrooms is red and has vein-like patterns that make it look like raw meat. The ovate spores are pink or ochre-colored.

Beefsteak Fungus

(24) Hen Of The Woods

Hen of the woods or grifola frondosa is an extremely delicious mushroom. These mushrooms are short-lived and smell pleasant until they are extremely mature.

Consuming them in small amounts is better because they can trigger allergic reactions. It is not always easy to spot these mushrooms because they grow in clusters almost the same color as the forest floor. They commonly grow in deciduous forests.

The fruiting body forms in tight clusters with wavy edges. Their caps can be quite large and are usually tan or grey-colored. The spores-bearing patches are present on the underside of the cap and, at times, even on the top. It has firm white flesh. Its ellipsoidal spores are white-colored.

Grifola Frondosa

(25) Chicken Of The Woods

Chicken of the woods or Laetiporus sulphureus is also known as the sulfur polypore.

These mushrooms are an excellent replacement for chicken due to their meaty texture. You will spot them in tier-like clusters on the stumps and trunks of oak, willow, chestnut, yew, and cherry trees. They do not have a discernible stem and grow in clusters.

The cap or flowering body can be up to 45 centimeters wide. Its globular fruiting body takes on a fan-like appearance when mature. The color also changes from sulphur yellow to ivory or pale yellow. Its flesh can be white or yellow-colored. Their ellipsoidal spores are white-colored.

Chicken of the woods or Laetiporus sulphureus

(26) Common Puffball

Common puffballs or Lycoperdon Perlatum are also known as wolf farts. These are extremely common mushrooms and are ideal for foragers who are just getting started.

They are usually found in mixed forests and pastures. Common puffballs typically grow in clusters but sometimes grow solitarily too.

The mushroom's average height and cap widths are 8 and 5 centimeters, respectively. These common mushrooms have a spherical body when young. As the mushroom grows, the cap takes on a club-like shape and is slightly flattened.

You will notice small triangular protrusions appearing in a net-like pattern. The color of its cap changes from white to cream or brown. The tapered club-like stem is white-colored and is covered in similar wart-like structures as the cap. The globose spores have fine warts on them and are olive or brown-colored.

Common puffballs or Lycoperdon Perlatum

(27) Parasol

Parasol mushroom or Macrolepiota Procera is relatively easy to identify and tastes good. These mushrooms are commonly found in pastures and open woods. The mushroom's average height and cap width are 40 and 30 centimeters, respectively.

It has a tan-colored cap that is round and bulbous when young. As the mushroom matures, it flattens and develops scales forming concentric circles. The white or cream-colored gills are crowded and free of the stem.

The stipe itself is white or off-white colored with a mottled snakeskin pattern. It has a thick double skirt that usually moves up and down along the length of the stem with a bulbous base. The ovoid spores are white-colored

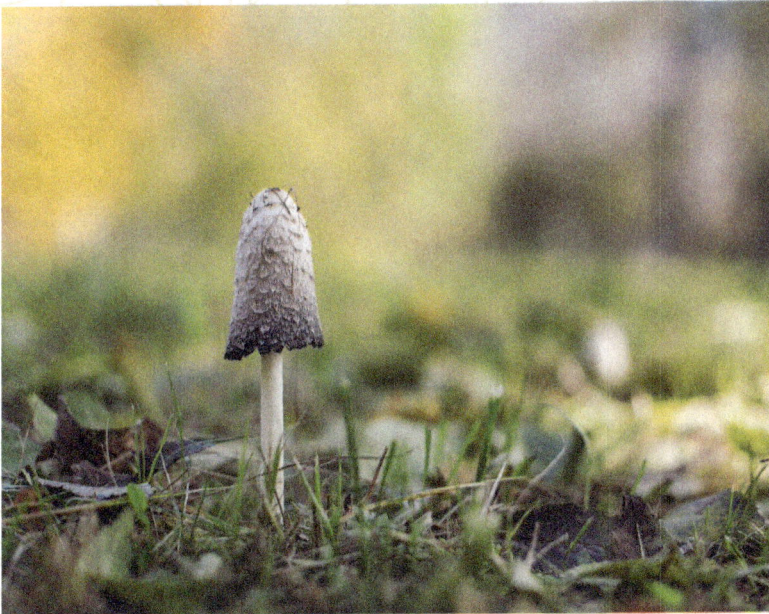

Parasol mushroom or Macrolepiota Procera

(28) Fairy Ring Champignons

Fairy ring champignons or Marasmius Oreades are also known as fairy ring mushrooms, Scotch bonnets, and elf rings. As the name suggests, these gourmet mushrooms appear in a ring-like fashion.

They are commonly found in the woods, pastures, lawns, and roadsides. The mushroom's average height and cap width are 8 and 5 centimeters, respectively. These common mushrooms have a convex or a conical cap flattens with maturity.

The pale tan-colored cap takes on a darker hue as it develops. The pale tan-colored gills are white, to begin with. These gills are free of the stem and are quite crowded. The stem is thin, tough, and fibrous and is off-white or tan. The ellipsoidal spores are white-colored.

Fairy ring champignons or Marasmius Oreades

(29) Yellow Morel

Yellow morel or Morchella Esculenta is also known as the common morel. These mushrooms taste delicious but are quite rare to spot.

Even though the name says common morels, they are not common. They grow toward the end of the field or open woods and pasture. These mushrooms prefer poorly alkaline soils. This mushroom has a honeycomb-like cap that is conical or oval-shaped.

It has irregular ridges and is hollow on the inside. The cap is joined to the stem at its very edge. The ridges are usually a lighter shade of yellow than the rest of the cap. The stem is ridged, too, and is white or cream-colored. It has uneven striations, is covered with a net-like mesh, and is hollow. These pleasant-smelling mushrooms have ellipsoidal or oval spores that are pale, cream, or yellow-colored.

Yellow morel or Morchella Esculenta
Image by Nadine Doerlé from Pixabay

(29) Black Morel

Black Morel or Morchella importuna are delicious mushrooms that should be consumed only after thoroughly cooked.

They can be found in urban areas as well as forests. They usually appear close to coniferous trees, wood chip beds and gardens, and any other disturbed grounds. The mushroom's average height and cap width are 10 and 5 centimeters, respectively.

These mushrooms also have a black honeycomb cap with parallel vertical ridges. The black color edges of the ridges are in stark contrast with the pale bits on the inside. These conical-shaped mushrooms are hollow and widen toward the bottom.

The stem is white or cream-colored and bruises brown or ochre. It has ridge-like structures on the outside and white flesh on the inside. These mushrooms have ellipsoidal cream-colored spores.

Black Morel or Morchella importuna

(30) Birch Polypore

Birch polypore or piptoporus betulinus it's also known as the razor strop fungus. It has white and firm flesh.

These mushrooms are commonly found on dead or damaged birch trees, hence their name. The mushroom's average height and cap width are 6 and 30 centimeters, respectively.

The subglobose cap of the mushroom takes on a hoof-like shape when fully mature. It also goes from white to grayish brown with age. In addition, these mushrooms have ellipsoidal and cylindrical white-colored pores.

This parasitic mushroom often kills its host Birch tree if it is not growing on dead trees.

(31) Grey Oyster Mushroom

Grey oyster mushroom or Pleurotus ostreatus gross across the UK throughout the year. These mushrooms are commonly found on deciduous trees, especially beech. They grow in shelf-like clusters and are extremely delicious.

The usual width of the cap is around 15 centimeters. They have convex shell-shaped caps when young. After the mushroom grows, the cap opens and flattens. It has irregular WAVY edges and is smoky brown or gray colored.

The white gills turn yellow as the mushroom matures. It has crowded gills that run along the length of the stem. The stem is white, and it might look like the mushrooms are coming straight out of the tree. They have cylindrical lilac-colored spores.

Birch Polypore or Piptoporus Betulinus

Grey oyster mushroom or Pleurotus ostreatus

(32) Butter Cap

Butter cap mushrooms or rhodocollybia are extremely common woodland mushrooms. They are edible but don't taste as good as the others discussed in this section.

The mushroom's average height and cap widths are 6 and 5 centimeters, respectively. The shape and the color of their cap change as the mushroom matures.

They start as convex and are almost black-colored. The caps lighten as the mushroom grows. The cap is usually flat, with a small peak in the center. It is smooth or greasy to the touch. The typically white gills are crowded and free of the stem. The white or off-white stem is long and narrow at the top. It can, at times, have a reddish-brown base too. They have ellipsoidal white or off-white/pink spores.

(33) Common Yellow Russula

Common Yellow Russula or Russula Ochroleuca is also known as yellow brittlegill. These tasty mushrooms are commonly found in mixed woodlands across the UK.

When it comes to foraging russulas, a simple rule is to always opt for yellow-caped variants. The only exception to this rule is the geranium-scented russula. As the name suggests, this toxic mushroom smells like geraniums.

Now, the familiar yellow russula is easy to identify. The mushroom's average height and cap width are 8 and 10 centimeters, respectively. The convex cap flattens as the mushrooms age.

It has a slight depression in the center. The cap can be yellow or tan colored. The stem is white or off-white depending on the stage of the mushroom's lifecycle. The stem is brittle to the touch and should snap like chalk.

The white or cream-colored gills are fairly crowded. They, too, are brittle like the stem. It has broad ovoid white or cream-colored spores.

Butter cap mushrooms or rhodocollybia

Common Yellow Russula or Russula Ochroleuca

Poisonous Mushrooms

Learning to identify edible mushrooms is not the only aspect of becoming a forager. It would help if you also learned about the common poisonous mushrooms you will encounter while foraging.

The toxicity of mushrooms varies from one species to another. Some might cause unpleasant symptoms that go away within a couple of hours, while others can be fatal.

So the simplest way to ensure you do not wrongly identify a specific mushroom is by learning about the poisonous variants. In the section, let's look at the most common toxic mushrooms you will encounter in the wild in the UK.

(1) Inky Cap

Inky cap or Agaricus Moelleri is quite a common mushroom across the UK, and it might look like the Prince mushroom at first. These mushrooms prefer woodlands but can be found in grasslands as well. The average height and width of the cap are 10 centimeters each.

Their usually white cap is covered with brown or smokey grey scales. The scales are dense in the center; therefore, the cap is darker in the middle. The cap usually starts with an oval shape and eventually becomes flat as the mushroom matures.

The pink gills on young mushrooms take on a black or a dark brown color when fully mature and are crowded. The stem is white and bulbous at the base. This mushroom also has a large pendulous skirt. The ellipsoidal spores are brown-colored.

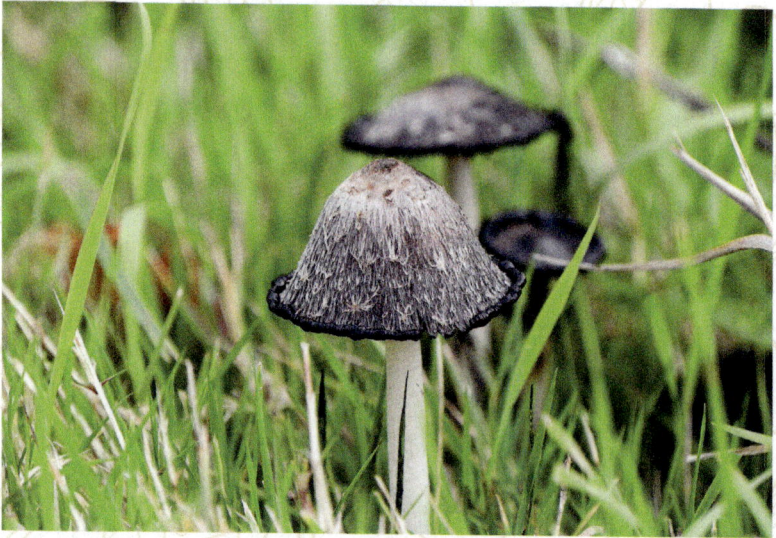

Inky cap or Agaricus Moelleri
Image by Freddy from Pixabay

(2) Gemmed Amanita

Gemmed amanita or amanita gemmata is also known as jeweled amanita.

These mushrooms prefer coniferous forests. The average height and width of the cap are 11 and 7 centimeters, respectively. The convex off-white cap becomes flat as the mushroom matures and takes on a pale yellow color.

You will notice small white pieces on the cap, which are the veil remnants. The crowded white gills are slightly connected to their white stem.

The stem might have a slightly yellow tinge as well. It is bulbous close to the base and is, at times, hollow in the middle. The ovoid spores are white-colored.

Gemmed Amanita or Amanita Gemmata

(3) Brown Roll Rim

Brown Roll Rim or Paxillus Involutus is a common roll rim and poison pax. These mushrooms prefer woodlands and broadleaved forests.

However, you might also find them near birch trees, grasslands, and lawns. The average height and width of the cap are 8 and 20 centimeters, respectively. Ensure you do not taste any part of this mushroom because it is poisonous. Their flattened caps are rusty brown colored with a slight depression in the center. The edges of the cap roll inward toward the gills. When wet, the cap looks slimy.

The crowded pale-yellow or dark-brown colored gills run down the length of the stem. The smooth and pale-brown stem turns a dark brown when bruised.

Its flesh is a pale yellowish-brown that darkens when bruised or cut. The ellipsoidal spores are brown-colored.

Brown Roll Rim or Paxillus Involutus

(4) Common Earthball

Common Earth Balls or Scleroderma Citrinum are also known as poison puffs, scaly earth balls, and leopard earth balls. These mushrooms prefer mossy or peat-rich soil and are commonly found in woodlands across the UK.

The average height and width of the cap are 8 and 12 centimeters, respectively. The fruiting body of these mushrooms is spherical, and the mushroom itself might look like a potato. There can be white, tan, or brown colors with darker wart-like coverings.

The skin is thick and leathery. It does not have a stem per se and, instead, has thread-like mycelial roots. The flesh of these mushrooms is purplish brown and can even be black at times.

The flesh has small white vein-like structures running through it. The globose spores are brown-colored with a mesh-like covering.

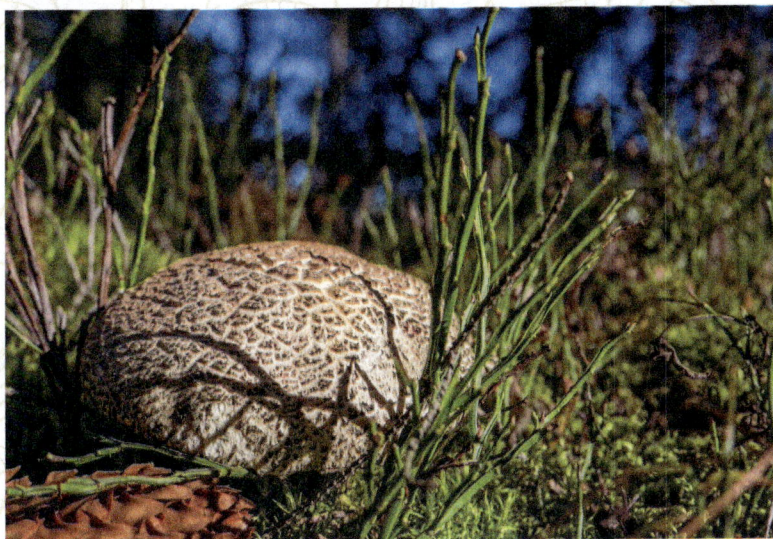

Common Earth Balls or Scleroderma Citrinum

(5) Clouded Agaric

Clouded agaric or Clitocybe Nebularis is also known as the clouded funnel mushroom. These mushrooms commonly grow in ring-like formations and are found under coniferous trees, deciduous forests, hedgerows, and grasslands in the UK. The average height and width of the cap are 12 and 20 centimeters, respectively.

The young mushrooms have a convex cap that eventually flattens out and looks like a shallow funnel, hence its name.

Its edges curl inward at later stages. Its usually tan-colored cap can be cloudy grey as well. The crowded gills run down the mushroom stem and go from white to yellow.

The fibrous off-white stem is slightly bulbous at the base. The ovoid or ellipsoidal spores are cream-colored.

Clouded agaric or Clitocybe Nebularis

(6) False Chanterelle

False Chanterelle or Hygrophoropsis Aurantiaca is not as poisonous as the others discussed in this section but causes various unpleasant symptoms upon consumption.

False chanterelles are commonly found in coniferous forests. The average height and width of the cap are 5 and 8 centimeters, respectively.

The initially convex-shaped cap forms a shallow funnel with a margin that rolls inward when mature. These mushrooms can be yellow with hues of orange and brown. The orange gills are forked, crowded, and run down the length of the stem.

The narrow stems are slightly tapered close to the base and are usually curved. The stem is the same color as the cap. Unlike edible chanterelles, these mushrooms don't have the typical apricot-like smell or the pristine white flesh. Its white spores are ellipsoidal.

False Chanterelle or Hygrophoropsis Aurantiaca

(7)Death Cap

A Death Cap or Amanita Phalloides can be easily mistaken for a giant puffball due to its convex cap when young. These mushrooms usually grow in mixed woodlands, especially deciduous trees. As the mushroom matures, the cap also opens and flattens out.

It takes on a green or olive color with tinges of yellow or tan in it. It becomes slimy to the touch when wet but looks shiny when dry. The average height and width of the cap are 15 and 12 centimeters, respectively.

The crowded cream or white-colored gills are free of the stem. The stem itself has a bulbous base and tapers toward the cap. This skirt has visible stations under it. The sub-globose or ellipsoidal spores are white-colored.

Death Cap or Amanita Phalloides

(8) False Morel

False Morel or Gyromitra Esculenta is a highly toxic mushroom that is unfit for consumption even when cooked. The simplest way to distinguish this from edible morels is by comparing their caps.

The average height and width of the cap are 5-10 and 4-14 centimeters, respectively. These mushrooms are commonly found in sandy soil, debris, and under pine trees.

These deadly but sweet-smelling mushrooms have convoluted and irregularly lobed caps. The cap looks like a tiny brain.

Unlike other mushrooms, the cap is connected to the stem at various points and hollow chambers are created on the inside.

Their color can be dark brown or orange, brown. The short white stem is bulbous toward the base and has hollow chambers inside.

60

False Morel or Gyromitra Esculenta

(9) Fly Agaric

Fly Agaric or Amanita Muscaria is quite pretty to look at and is something right out of a storybook. However, it is poisonous, and you should stay away from it. These mushrooms can be commonly found in mixed woodlands but have a preference for birch trees.

The average height and width of the cap are 20 and 25 centimeters, respectively. The cap of young mushrooms is hemispherical but slowly opens out and becomes flat as the mushroom matures. The color also changes from orange to bright red. The bright red cap is covered with white-yellow scales that are the remnants of the veil.

The fairly crowded gills are white-cream colored and are not joined to the stem.

61

This stem has a bulbous base. It is not smooth and shaggy due to the remnants of the volva. The large pendulous white or off-white skirt has yellow edges. The ellipsoidal spores are white.

Fly Agaric or Amanita Muscaria

Image by Andreas from Pixabay

(10) Yellow Stainer

The Yellow Stainer or Agaricus Xanthodermus is a poisonous mushroom that can cause unpleasant symptoms but might not affect everyone. That said, it is better to stay away from this mushroom. These mushrooms are commonly found in open forests, hedgerows, and grasslands. They form in clusters or rings.

The average height and cap width of these mushrooms are 16 centimeters each. The round and white-colored cap flattens and takes on a shallow convex shape as the mushroom matures. It has very tiny scales on it.

The cap of this mushroom stains yellow when bruised, hence its name. The crowded white gills take on a grey-brown hue when fully mature. Its white or off-white stem has a pendulous skirt and a bulbous base. The ellipsoidal or ovoid spores are purple or brown colored.

Yellow Stainer or Agaricus Xanthodermus

4. Preserving and Storing Mushrooms

Mushrooms are a part of different culinary traditions across the globe. The texture and taste of most mushrooms can quickly elevate any dish you are cooking. Their earthy aroma and taste make them an ideal pairing for meat-based dishes. These nutritious ingredients could soon boost your meal's flavor and nutrient profile.

An important aspect of becoming a forager is not just learning to forage mushrooms. After all, what is the point of spending hours searching for mushrooms if you don't enjoy them? This is where the concept of cooking and preserving mushrooms steps into the picture.

Foraging Mushroom

Preserving Mushroom

Whether it is a soup, pasta, stew, or salad, fresh mushrooms can be added to various dishes. Most taste incredible when sautéed with a bit of butter and aromatics or grilled and fried.

Regardless of the recipe, you want to experiment with, ensure that you always cook the mushroom before eating. Mushrooms should never be consumed in their raw form.

 Even though certain species can be eaten right away, it's always better to cook them. This is because mushrooms have rigid cellular walls that are indigestible when uncooked. Also, the nutrients present in mushrooms break free easily and offer better absorption of the vitamins and minerals present when exposed to heat.

Apart from this, any natural toxins, allergens, or irritants present in the mushrooms are also eliminated when cooked.

If you are trying a specific mushroom for the first time, it's better that you do not drink alcohol. This is especially true for certain mushroom varieties discussed in this book. Alcohol may trigger a stronger allergic reaction to mushrooms, especially those of the Coprinus genus (commonly known as shaggy mane mushrooms).

Ideally, avoid consuming mushrooms three days before or after drinking alcohol. It might trigger unpleasant symptoms such as vomiting, nausea, sweating, diarrheal, and palpitations.

Ensure that you thoroughly clean the mushrooms before you start cooking with them.

This is crucial for any foods that have been foraged in the wild. The smooth skin-like surface of mushrooms is waterproof; therefore, most species can be washed without a problem. However, if the specific variety of mushrooms you are handling is absorbent, cleaning it for prolonged periods is not a good idea because it tends to lose flavor and become soggy when placed in water. Instead, a soft-bristled brush helps eliminate the dirt and debris to preserve its crispness. After this, a soft wet cloth can clean the dirty surface.

Mushroom cleaning by water

If you have foraged more mushrooms than you can consume them right away or want to store some, preserving them is crucial. The ideal way to keep mushrooms is by dehydrating or freezing them.

Certain mushrooms are suited for canning and pickling as well. Ideally, dehydrating the mushrooms ensures their aroma and flavors stay intact. They can also be rehydrated when added to soups and pasta. Dried mushrooms can also be turned into powders that can be used as a seasoning. You don't need any special air-drying equipment. Instead, clean the mushrooms, and hang them to dry in a room or an area with sufficient airflow. If you have a dehydrator, it makes the entire process quicker.

Canned Mushroom

Pickled Mushroom

Mushroom Powder

Two options are available for storing mushrooms, and they are freezing and drying.

Both are commonly used and work well for most species of mushrooms. Once the mushrooms are dried, place them in an airtight jar or a plastic bag to prolong their shelf life.

If the mushrooms are sliced too thinly or crushed finely, vacuum sealing might not work. Once you have placed the mushrooms in airtight containers, ensure they are vacuum-sealed.

Dried mushrooms can be stored between 6-12 months when appropriately sealed.

The other option that can be used for preserving mushrooms is freezing. This does not alter their fiber or calorie content. However, the texture is slightly altered due to their high water content affected by freezing.

Some mushrooms can become mushy or softer when frozen and thawed. So, if you want to use frozen mushrooms, they are well suited for soups, stews, and curries instead of any recipe that calls for sautéing. Freezing mushrooms is quite convenient. You simply need to place the cleaned mushrooms in an airtight bag such as a ziplock bag and place them in a freezer. These can last anywhere between 6-12 months when stored properly.

5. Let's Cook - Wild Mushroom Recipes

Note: Clean the mushrooms very well after harvesting them. Wipe them with a moist paper towel. If soil is stuck on them, rinse the mushrooms.

(1) Beefsteak Mushrooms with Wood Sorrel

Serves: 2

Ingredients:
- 6 ounces fresh beefsteak mushrooms, cut into ¼ inch slices on a mandolin slicer
- 2 large cloves of garlic, lightly crushed
- Salt to taste.
- ¼ cup thickly shredded or chopped wood sorrel
- 6 tablespoons extra-virgin olive oil or walnut oil
- 2 small sprigs of rosemary, bruised
- 2 teaspoons fresh lemon juice
- Wood sorrel flowers to garnish

Directions:

- Pour oil into a pan. Add garlic and rosemary and place the pan over medium heat. When the oil is hot and garlic and rosemary are lightly browned, turn off the heat.
- Remove the garlic and rosemary if desired.
- Add mushrooms, salt, wood sorrel, and lemon juice and mix well.

- Transfer into a bowl. Garnish with wood sorrel flowers and serve. You can make this ahead of time and place it in the refrigerator but make sure to use it in 5 days. Freshly cooked mushrooms will be crisp but the leftovers (or made ahead) will be softer.

Beefsteak Mushrooms with Wood Sorrel

(2) Pan Fried Oyster Mushrooms

Serves: 2

Ingredients:

- ½ pound oyster mushrooms, cut into large pieces (discard stems if desired)
- 2 cloves garlic, unpeeled, crushed
- Salt to taste
- 1 tablespoon butter
- 1 green onion, chopped
- Black pepper to taste

Directions:

- Add butter into a skillet. Place the skillet over medium-high heat. When butter melts, add mushrooms into the pan and spread them evenly all over the pan. Now do not stir until the underside is golden brown. Flip the mushrooms and add garlic, pepper, salt, and green onions and stir. Now cook until the mushrooms are golden brown on the underside.

- Mix well and turn off the heat. Remove the mushroom mixture into a bowl and serve.

Pan Fried Oyster Mushrooms

(3) Field Mushroom Soup

Serves: 2

Ingredients

- 1 pound field mushrooms, scrape the skin, coarsely chopped
- 1 chicken stock cube
- 2 small garlic cloves, peeled, crushed, finely chopped
- ½ vegetable stock cube
- 1 medium onion, chopped
- 2 cups water

Directions:

- Pour water into a saucepan and place the saucepan over medium heat. When water starts boiling, add mushrooms, onion, chicken, and vegetable stock cubes and stir.

- Cook on low heat for about 30 minutes. Turn off the heat. Blend with an immersion blender until smooth.

- Pour into bowls and serve.

72

(4) Baked Giant Puffball Mushroom and Italian Salsa Verde

Serves: 8

Ingredients:

- ½ giant puffball mushroom
- ½ cup cream
- Salt to taste
- Oil to fry
- 4 eggs
- ¼ cup flour
- ¼ cup white breadcrumbs
- Pepper to taste

For salsa Verde:
- 2 bunches parsley, chopped
- 4 cloves garlic, peeled, sliced
- 2 tablespoons capers
- 4 teaspoons mustard
- 1 cup olive oil
- 1 onion, chopped
- 2 small leeks, chopped
- 4 pickled gherkins, chopped
- Salt to taste
- 4 tablespoons white wine vinegar
- Pepper to taste

Baked Giant Puffball

Directions:

- Place flour on a plate and breadcrumbs on another plate. Crack eggs into a bowl. Add cream, salt, and pepper and whisk well.
- First, roll the mushroom slices in flour, one at a time. Next, dunk in egg mixture and finally dredge in breadcrumbs. Place on a plate.
- Pour enough oil into a deep pan (about 2 inches in height from the bottom of the pan) and place the pan over medium heat. Let the oil heat to 365 degrees F.
- Meanwhile, make salsa Verde: Combine parsley, garlic, capers, mustard, onions, leeks, gherkins, salt, pepper, and vinegar in a bowl.
- Blend with an immersion blender pouring oil simultaneously while blending.
- Blend until the consistency you desire is achieved.

- Carefully slide a few breaded mushrooms into the hot oil. Do not crowd the pan and cook them in batches.
- Cook until golden brown and crisp, turning occasionally. Remove mushrooms with a slotted spoon and place them on a plate lined with paper towels.
- Season the mushrooms with salt and pepper. Serve crispy mushrooms with salsa Verde.

(5)Turkey Scallopini with Fava Beans and Wild Mushrooms

Serves: 6 – 8

Ingredients:

- 3 pounds turkey tenderloins, cut into 2-ounce medallions
- 12 – 16 ounces edible wild mushrooms of your choice
- 2 cups meat stock
- 2 tablespoons cooking oil of your choice
- Kosher salt to taste
- Freshly ground pepper to taste
- 2 2/3 cups shucked, blanched, peeled fava beans or English peas
- 1 cup dry white wine

- ½ cup diced shallot (¼ inch dice)

- ½ cup unsalted butter

- ½ cup all-purpose flour or more if required

Directions:

- Place turkey slices between 2 sheets of plastic sheet and pound with a meat mallet until the slices are ¼ inch thick. Keep them aside.

- Sprinkle salt and pepper over the turkey scallopini and roll them in flour. Shake off the excess flour and keep them on a plate.

- Place a large skillet over medium heat. Add about 1 tablespoon of oil. When the oil is hot, place about half the turkey scallopini in the pan. Do not crowd the pan. Cook until the underside is brown. Turn the slices over and cook the other side until brown.

- Remove the turkey with a slotted spoon and place it on a plate. Cook the remaining turkey slices adding the remaining oil. Make sure you do not crowd the pan so you can cook them in 3 batches if required.

- Cover the plate with foil and place it in an oven to keep warm.

- To make the mushroom sauce, drain the fat from the pan and add ½ the butter into the pan. When butter melts, add mushrooms and cook until light brown.

- Add salt to taste. When shallots are light brown, pour wine into the pan. Cook until the wine is half its original quantity.

-

- Pour stock and cook until it is half the original quantity. Add 3 tablespoons butter and whisk well. Cook until the sauce is thick. Turn off the heat and keep warm.

- In the meantime, place a pan over medium-low heat. Add remaining butter and let it melt.

- Add fava beans and salt and stir. Let it cook for a few minutes. Once they are tender, turn off the heat.

- Combine half the mushroom sauce and turkey scallopini.

- To serve: Divide turkey scallopini into 6 – 8 plates. Scatter fava beans on top. Spoon the remaining sauce over the beans on each plate and serve.

Turkey Scallopini with Fava Beans and Wild Mushrooms

(6)Pavement Mushroom Toast

Serves: 2

Ingredients:

- pounds pavement mushrooms, chopped into large chunks

- 2 cloves garlic

- 1 cup double cream

- A handful of chopped parsley to garnish

- 3.5 ounces butter

- 2 sprigs thyme

- 1 cup vegetable stock

- 4 slices of bread, toasted

- Salt to taste

- Pepper to taste

Directions:

- Add half the butter into a pan and let it melt over medium heat. When butter melts, add garlic and thyme and cook until garlic turns light golden brown. Stir often. Stir in the mushrooms and cook until brown. Stir often. Discard any of the cooked fat from the pan.

- Add stock and cream and let it come to a boil. Lower the heat and simmer until thick. Add salt and pepper and stir.

- Butter the toasted bread slices. Spoon the mushroom sauce over the bread slices. Garnish with parsley and serve.

Pavement Mushroom Toast
Photo by Lottie Griffiths on Unsplash

(7) Wild Mushroom Conserve

Serves: 2

Ingredients:

- 4-pound small chanterelle mushrooms
- 1 cup canola oil or neutral flavored oil

- 1 cup water
- 4 teaspoons chopped fresh thyme
- 6 cloves garlic, peeled, thinly sliced
- 2 teaspoons kosher salt
- 1 cup white wine or apple cider vinegar
- 4 dried bay leaves

Directions:

- You need to clean these mushrooms with cold water. Spread them on layers of paper towels over a baking sheet.

- Let them drain for an hour or so.

- Place a soup pot over medium heat. Add garlic and cook until golden brown, making sure not to burn the garlic.

- Stir in salt, mushrooms, and thyme. Keep the pan covered and cook until the mushrooms release the juices and shrink in size.

- Pour water and vinegar. When the mixture starts boiling, remove mushrooms with a slotted spoon and place in 2 jars of 1 quart each.

- Let the liquid in the pot boil for a couple of minutes. Turn off the heat. Pour the boiling liquid into the jars. The mushrooms should be covered in the liquid so press the mushrooms into the jar.

- Fasten the lid and place them in water for 15 minutes. Once you use mushrooms from a jar, place that jar in the refrigerator.

(8) St. George's Mushroom on Toast Wild Garlic Pesto

Serves: 4

Ingredients:

- 14 ounces St. George's mushrooms or oyster mushrooms or chestnut mushrooms
- 2 cloves garlic, minced
- 2 tablespoons butter
- Pepper to taste
- 8 slices sourdough bread, toasted

- 1 teaspoon chopped fresh thyme or ½ teaspoon dried thyme
- 2 teaspoons balsamic vinegar
- Salt to taste

For wild garlic pesto:

- 1 heaping cup of chopped wild garlic
- 1 ½ tablespoons nutritional yeast
- ½ clove garlic, peeled
- Salt to taste
- 3 tablespoons pine nuts
- 1/8 cup olive oil
- ½ tablespoon lemon juice

Directions:

- To pesto: Blend together wild garlic, nutritional yeast, garlic, salt, pine nuts, and lemon juice in a blender until smooth. With the blender running, pour oil in a thin drizzle and blend until well combined. Pour into a bowl.

- Add butter into a pan and let it melt over medium heat. Add garlic and cook until brown.

- Stir in mushrooms and thyme and cook until tender. Stir in seasonings and vinegar and cook until nearly dry.

- Smear a little pesto on each bread slice. Spread mushrooms on each toast. Spoon some pesto on top and serve. Store leftover pesto in the refrigerator and use it within 4 days.

St. George's Mushroom or Calocybe Gambosa

St. George's Mushroom on Toast

(9)Fried Black Morel

Serves: 4 – 6

Ingredients:

- 1.8 pounds black morel, halved or quartered depending on the size
- Salt to taste
- 1 teaspoon chopped parsley (optional)
- 3.5 ounces butter
- Pepper to taste

Directions:

- Add butter into a large pan and let it melt over medium heat. Once butter melts, add pepper, salt, and mushrooms and cover the pan.

- Cook for about 5 minutes or until water is released. Stir often.

- Uncover and cook until dry and the butter start browning. Garnish with parsley and serve.

Fried Black Morel

(10)Orange Peel Fungus Soup

Serves: 8

Ingredients:

- 2 cups dried cannellini beans or great Northern beans soaked in water overnight
- 2/3 cup cracked wheat or buckwheat groats
- 8 cups fresh Orange Peel Fungus mushroom
- Salt to taste
- Pepper to taste
- ½ cup sour cream
- Sliced green onion to garnish
- ½ cup chopped onion
- ½ cup chopped celery
- ½ cup chopped carrot
- 8 cups savoy or green onion, cut into ½-inch square pieces
- 2 bay leaves
- ½ cup vodka
- Oil to cook, as required
- 10 cups water
- Freshly ground pepper to garnish

Directions:

- Peel the mushroom caps and cut them into 2 halves. Cut each half into ½-inch thick slices. Cut the stems into ½-inch thick round slices.

- Pour about 4 – 5 tablespoons of oil into a soup pot and place the pot over medium heat. When the oil is hot, add the mushrooms and cook until dry. Add salt to taste.

- Meanwhile, blend together onion, celery, and carrot in a blender until smooth.

- Pour the blended vegetables into the pot and cook until nearly dry.

- Stir in cabbage, water, beans, bay leaves, and cracked wheat. When the mixture starts boiling, lower the heat and cook for an hour or until the beans are cooked.

- Add salt and pepper to taste.

- While the soup is cooking, pour vodka into a small pan. Place the pan over medium heat. Light it up (vodka) with a matchstick or a lighter, and turn off the heat.

- Soon the fire will die down, and you should have about 2 tablespoons of vodka remaining in the pan. Pour the vodka into the sour cream. Add salt and pepper to taste.

- To serve: Ladle the soup into soup bowls. Drizzle some sour cream mixture on top.

- Garnish with green onions and some freshly ground pepper, and serve.

6. Seasonal Calendar– UK Mushrooms

An often-overlooked factor used for identifying mushrooms is the season. Most mushrooms grow only during specific months.

In the previous chapter, you were introduced to different edible and poisonous mushrooms commonly found in the UK. In this chapter, let's look at the common months during which these mushrooms are found.

Edible Mushrooms

Name	Commonly Found During
Horse mushroom	August – October
The prince	August – October
Pavement mushroom	May – October
Medusa mushroom	July – October

Field mushroom	July – October
Scaly wood mushroom	June – October
The blushing wood mushroom	May – November
Wood mushroom	August – November
Orange peel fungus	August – November
Orange grisette	July – October
The blusher	June – October
Grisettes	June – November
Honey fungus	August – November

Wood ears	Throughout the year
Butter bolete	July – October
Peppery bolete	August – October
Summer bolete	June – August
Giant puffball	July – September
Chanterelle	June – November
Winter chanterelle	August – December
Shaggy ink cap	July – November
Horn of plenty	August – October

Beefsteak fungus	July – October
Hen of the woods	July – October
Chicken of the woods	May – August
Common puffball	July – October
Parasol	July – October
Fairy ring champignons	April – November
Yellow morel	March – May
Black morel	March – May
Birch polypore	August – November

Grey oyster mushroom	Throughout the year
Butter cap	July – December
Common yellow russula	September – November

Poisonous Mushrooms

Name	Commonly Found During
Inky cap	June – October
Gemmed amanita	May – November
Brown roll rim	August – November
Common earth ball	September – November

Poisonous Mushrooms

Clouded agaric	September – December
False chanterelle	August – November
Death cap	August – September
False morel	March – May
Fly agaric	August – November

How to harvest mushrooms correctly?

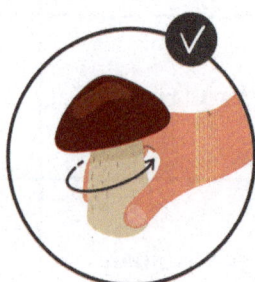

7. Conclusion

I want to thank you once again for choosing this book. I hope it proved to be an enjoyable and informative read!

If you reside anywhere in England, Scotland, Wales, or Northern Ireland, do not let go of any opportunities to forage mushrooms in the wild.

Foraging for mushrooms is an exciting, rewarding, and relaxing activity. All you need is the right information. With a little patience, an open mind to learn, and the right source of information, you can become an efficient mushroom forager.

 The general climatic conditions in the UK create the perfect ecosystem that sustains the growth of different species of mushrooms.

To start foraging edible mushrooms, follow the four simple steps discussed in this book. This and a little commitment to learning are the only two things needed to start foraging ethically.

Spend some time and acquaint yourself with the different species of mushrooms included in this book. Always carry the required tools to identify and harvest mushrooms, such as a magnifying glass on a pocketknife.

Also, ensure that you are certain of the mushroom you are harvesting before you go ahead and do it.

Certain edible mushrooms are scrumptious, while others have healing properties.

Unless you learn about them, you cannot make the most of the different benefits they offer. This is also needed to ensure you are not harvesting inedible or poisonous mushrooms.

This book will act as your guide every step of the way. All the information you need about understanding the basics of mushrooms and foraging them in the wild is included here. Planning, preparation, and the right information, coupled with a little dedication, are all that is needed. Also, it's not just about learning, ensure that you start using the information given in this book to improve your skills as a forager.

Apart from all this, spend some time exploring the different recipes in this book using wild edible mushrooms. Once you learn to forage mushrooms, ensure you enjoy your foraging efforts.

Now, all left for you is to start using the information given in this book and forage edible mushrooms in the UK! Also, there is no time like the present to start this endeavor!

Thank you, and all the best!

EDIBLE MUSHROOMS SET

CEP

CHAMPIGNONS

AGARIC

OYSTER

SUILLUS

CORAL MILKY CAR

PORCINI

RUSSULA

LACTARIUS

ASPEN

CAESAR'S

MOREL

SAFFRON

SHIITAKE

CHANTERELLE

BLACK TRUFFLE

ENOKI

INDIGO LACTARIUS

LION'S MANE MUSHROOM

PUFFBALL

Appendix - 2- Spore Print

Cut off stem → Put cap on white paper → Remove cap
Wait a few hours...

The Mushroom

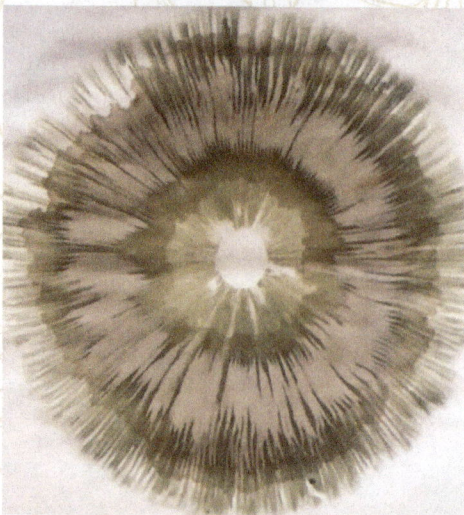
Spore Print

Appendix - 2- Identification Logbook

General Details

📅 _____
Date/Day

☀️ ☐   🌤️☁️ ☐   🌧️ ☐
Weather

📍 _____
Location/GPS

🌡️ _____
Temprature

👤 _____
By/Person

Growth Medium & Surrounding

 ☐ Coniferous   ☐ Tropical   ☐ Deciduous   ☐ Others

Forest Type   Remarks _____

   ☐ Soil   ☐ Grass   ☐ Dead Wood   ☐ Tree

☐ Leaf   ☐ Rocky Surface   ☐ Mushroom   ☐ Other

Growth Medium

Remarks _____

   ☐ Clay   ☐ Sandy   ☐ Loam   ☐ Others

Soil Type

Additional Information

Species/Type _____   Color _____

Specimen _____   Length _____

- [ ] Conical
- [ ] Bell
- [ ] Funnel
- [ ] Umbonate
- [ ] Flat

- [ ] Hemispherical
- [ ] Umblicate
- [ ] Convex
- [ ] Oval
- [ ] Depression

- [ ] Conical Scale
- [ ] Knobbed
- [ ] Sunken
- [ ] Kidney
- [ ] Cone shaped revoluted

- [ ] sessile
- [ ] Helm
- [ ] Sub-globular
- [ ] Papillate
- [ ] Dimidiate

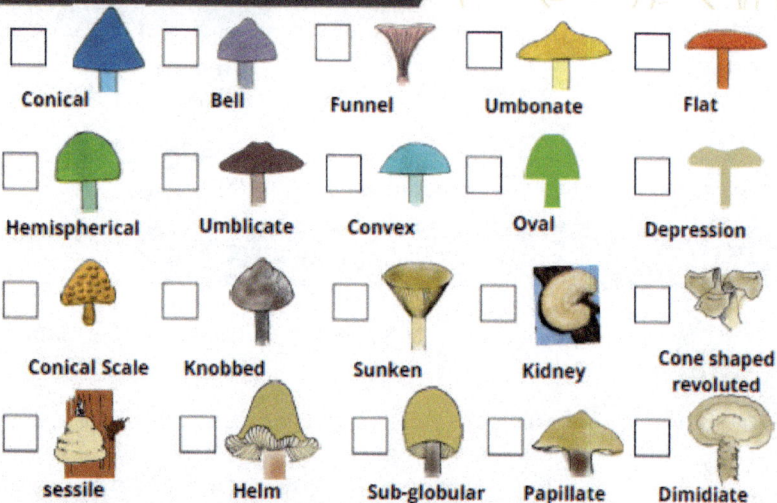

Additional Cap Information

Cap Diagram	Other details	
	Cap color	....
	Cap shape	....
	Cap texture	....
	Cap diameter	....
	Cap length	....
	Hymenium	....

Cap surface

- [ ] Smooth
- [ ] Pathces
- [ ] Flat scales
- [ ] Velvet
- [ ] Hairy

Gills

- [ ] False Gills
- [ ] Teeth
- [ ] Pores
- [ ] Gills

- [ ] Close
- [ ] Spaced
- [ ] Intermediate
- [ ] Anastomosing

Additional Notes

Gill attachment to the stalk

Example of free gill attachment

☐ **Free**
(Not attached)

☐ **Adnexed**
(Narrowly attached)

☐ **Sinuate**
(Notched before slightly running down)

☐ **Subdecurrent**
(Gills running slightly down the stem)

☐ **Emarginate**
Notched before attachment

☐ **Adnate**
Widely attached

☐ **Decurrent**
(Running down)

☐ **Seceding**
(Gills attached but breaking away)

Sketch

Additional Notes

☐ Equal   ☐ Club shaped   ☐ Bulbous   ☐ Volva (with cup)   ☐ Rooting

☐ With rhizoids   ☐ Tapering downwards   ☐ Tapering upwards   ☐ Dub shaped

Mushroom Ring Type

☐ Pendant   ☐ Ring zone   ☐ Cobwebby   ☐ Double

Sketch

☐ Flaring   ☐ Sheathing

REFERENCES

Foraging: Ultimate Guide to Wild Food. (n.d.). Foraging for
Wild Edibles.
https://www.wildedible.com/foraging#:~:text=Use%20all%20
of%20your%20senses.&text=Lots%20of%20wild%20edible%2
0

Hale, J. (2016, May 25). Can you identify the poisonous plants
of the Pacific Northwest? Oregonlive.
https://www.oregonlive.com/travel/2016/05/can_you_identif
y_the_poisonous.html

Kloos, S. (2017, April 13). Wildcrafting Basics: Toxic Plants. The
School of Forest Medicine.
https://forestmedicine.net/ecological-intelligence-
blog/2017/4/10/toxic-plants

Maxey, L. (2018, August 9). Foraging as a Route to Wellbeing.
Network of Wellbeing.
https://networkofwellbeing.org/2018/08/09/foraging-as-a-
route-to-wellbeing/

Ovenden, S. (n.d.). Foraging: A beginner's guide. BBC Good
Food. https://www.bbcgoodfood.com/howto/guide/foraging

Rezackova, L. (2020, July 2). 7 Amazing Benefits of Foraging for
Wild Foods. Creativeedgetravel.
https://www.creativeedgetravel.com/post/7-amazing-
benefits-of-foraging-for-wild-foods

MR. FLEMING'S

PACIFIC NORTHWEST EDIBLE PLANT FORAGING & MUSHROOM FIELD GUIDE

A complete Pacific Northwest Foraging Guide with 50+ Wild Plants & Mushrooms, 18+ Recipes & 150+ Instructional Colored Images

DIY MUSHROOM SERIES

MR. FLEMING'S

HOW TO GROW AND USE GOURMET & MEDICINAL MUSHROOMS

A Mushroom Field Guide with Step-by-Step Instructions and Images for Mushroom Identification, Cultivation, Usage and Recipes

DIY MUSHROOM SERIES

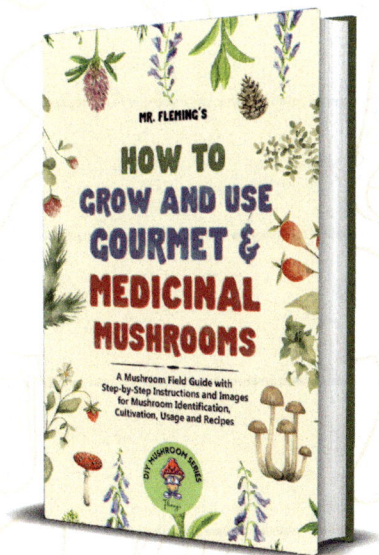

We'd Love Your Feedback!

⭐ ⭐ ⭐ ⭐ ⭐

Please let us know how we're doing by leaving us a review.

Notes

Notes

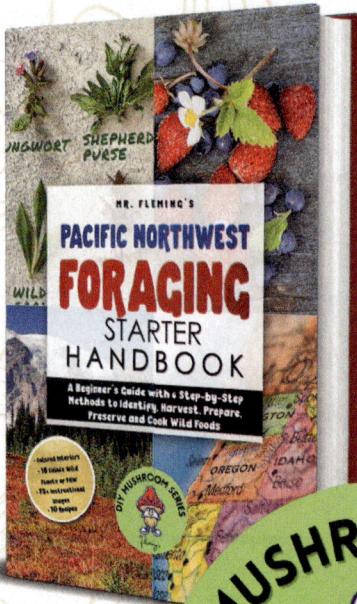

MR. FLEMING'S

PACIFIC NORTHWEST
FORAGING
STARTER
HANDBOOK

A Beginner's Guide with a Step-by-Step
Methods to Identify, Harvest, Prepare,
Preserve and Cook Wild Foods

DIY MUSHROOM SERIES

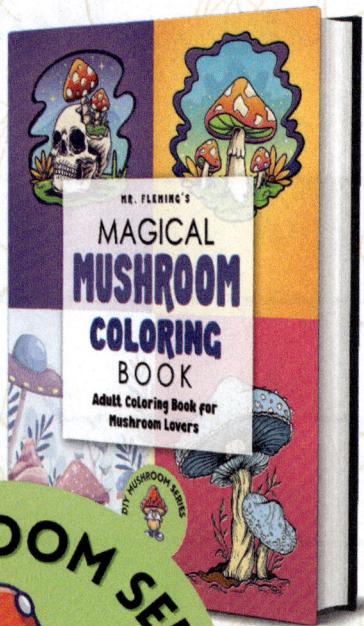

MR. FLEMING'S

MAGICAL
MUSHROOM
COLORING
BOOK

Adult Coloring Book for
Mushroom Lovers

DIY MUSHROOM SERIES

DIY MUSHROOM SERIES

Fleming's

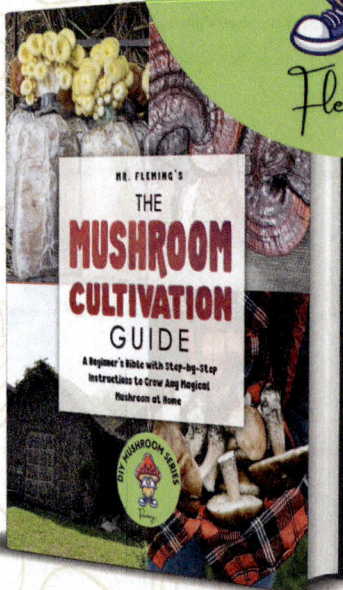

MR. FLEMING'S

THE
MUSHROOM
CULTIVATION
GUIDE

A Beginner's Bible with Step-by-Step
Instructions to Grow Any Magical
Mushroom at Home

DIY MUSHROOM SERIES

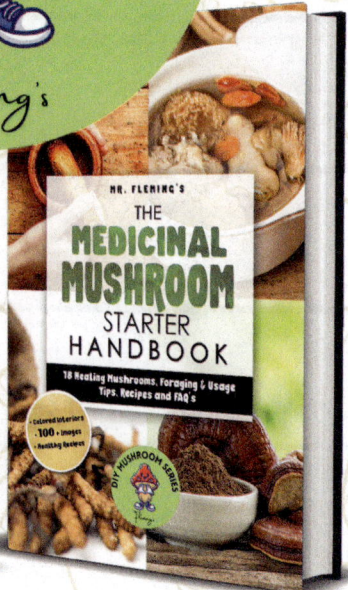

MR. FLEMING'S

THE
MEDICINAL
MUSHROOM
STARTER
HANDBOOK

18 Healing Mushrooms, Foraging & Usage
Tips, Recipes and FAQ's

DIY MUSHROOM SERIES

Printed in Great Britain
by Amazon